ISBN 978-0-260-53781-2
PIBN 10954782

THE Demand and Price SITUATION

BUREAU OF AGRICULTURAL ECONOMICS
UNITED STATES DEPARTMENT OF AGRICULTURE
WASHINGTON, D. C. BAE JUNE 1945

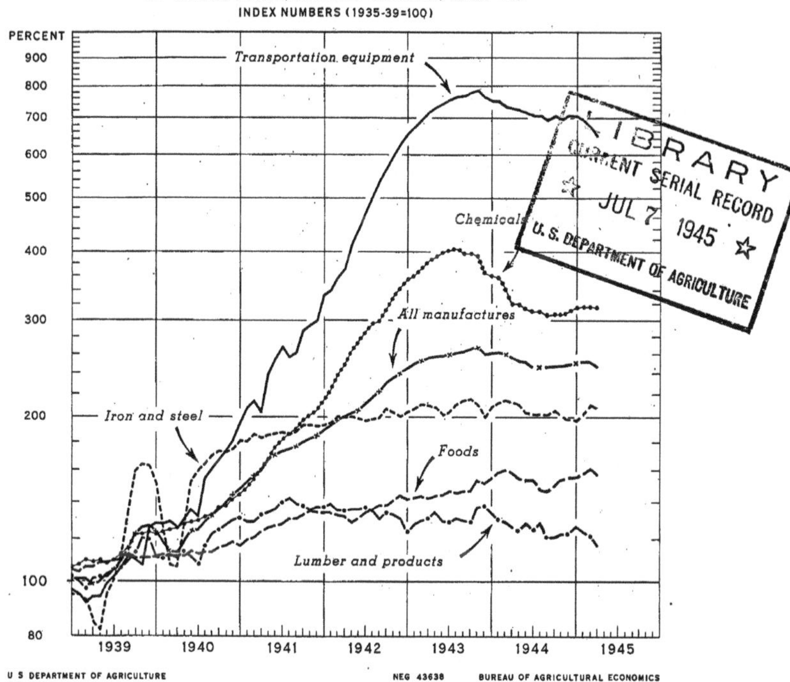

There was a very large increase in the output of manufactures from 1939 to the end of 1943 declined slightly in the next 6 months, and then remained nearly stable until VE day.

The largest declines since the end of 1943 have been in transportation equipment and in chemicals which also increased the most in the earlier part of the war. Aircraft and ship building are included as part of transportation equipment, and explosives and ammunition as part of chemicals. The production of iron and steel, which provides the raw material for much of the transportation equipment, more than doubled by late 1943 and in April 1945 was only 3 percent below its peak. The processing of foods was larger in 1944 and early 1945 than in any previous year.

THE DEMAND AND PRICE SITUATION

CONTENTS

DEMAND FOR FARM PRODUCTS

The demand for farm products is likely to remain sufficiently high during the remainder of 1945 and the early months of 1946, to take the available suppli of most products at or near current prices. The present civilian demand is such that substantially larger quantities of many products would be purchased if they were available. Consequently, a moderate reduction in consumer incomes will not result in a corresponding decline in prices or quantities purcashed. Also, the Government will continue to purchase very large quantities of farm products for t armed forces and for relief purposes, and such purchases will not be affected by changes in civilian purchasing power.

Reduction in the production of munitions and other war goods as a result of the end of the war in Europe were relatively small in May and early June, but are expected to become much larger in the next few months. The reductions that may be expected within a year, assuming that the war with Japan does not end within that time, might vary from 25 to 50 percent. Munitions production during the first 3 months of 1945 was at an annual rate of about 52 billion dollars. Approximately 9 million persons were employed in such production.

If the output of munitions should be reduced by one-third by the first quarter of 1946, the annual rate of expenditures of the Government would be reduced by about 16 billion dollars. Employment, assuming no change in the output per worker, would be reduced by 3 million persons. Of course, Government expenditures other than for munitions would also decline, because of the reduction in the size of the Army and the curtailment of various other Government activities connected with the war. The War Department has estimated that the size of the Army will be reduced by about 1.3 million men during the year following VE day. This is a reduction of about 16 percent in the size of the Army or 11 percent of all armed forces. No reduction in the size of the Navy is expected.

There are no estimates of the number of persons whose employment might be affected by other reductions in Government activity, but it seems reasonable to expect that the total in all categories might reach at least 5 million. This would be equal to about 8 percent of the present total labor force, including persons in the armed forces, or 10 percent of the number of civilians employed during the first quarter of 1945.

This does not mean that that many persons would become unemployed, even temporarily. In most industries, part of the reduction in the amount of labor needed would be met by the reduction or elimination of overtime. Average weekly hours worked in industries producing durable manufactured goods increased nearly one-fourth during the war. Some of the employees formerly producing munitions would be immediately transferred to the production of civilian goods or the work of reconverting plants for such production. A good many workers who do lose their jobs because of reduced production of war goods will soon obtain employment in industries serving the civilian market, although perhap at lower wages. Many such workers will receive unemployment compensation during the time they are temporarily unemployed. Such compensation will hel to maintain the demand for farm products.

The wartime labor force in the United States is larger than normal, because of the employment of many persons who would not have taken jobs in normal times. The number so employed during the first quarter of 1945 may easily have been at least 5 million. Of course not all of these people will wish to leave the labor force during the year following VE day. But some of them, such as the wives of discharged soldiers and persons of normal retirement age, will wish to quit working. Consequently, the decline in civilian employment probably will be somewhat greater than the increase in unemployme

The effect of these shifts will be different in various parts of the United States. In areas where there was a considerable increase in populati because of the establishment of war industries, a significant amount of unemployment may appear and workers will need to move elsewhere to obtain emp ment. This will be particularly true of areas where the industries cannot readily converted to the production of civilian goods. Areas where shipbui ing and airplane manufacture are important and where there are no other ind tires capable of employing large numbers may experience the greatest difficu in the reconversion period.

Declines in the production of war goods will be partly offset by increases in the production of civilian goods during the coming year. This largely take the form of increased production of durable consumers' goods, as automobiles and household equipment. The extent to which the production such goods offsets the reduction in war goods will probably depend more on available supplies of raw materials than on the extent of consumer demand, since the deferred demand for such articles is very large.

The net result of declines in war production and increases in output of civilian goods will doubtless be a decline in total output and in income payments received by individuals. The extent of the decline in income payments from the first quarter of 1945 to the first quarter of 1946 does not seem likely to exceed 10 percent, if the present price level is maintained. This would mean that income payments in early 1946 would be about equivalent to those of the latter part of 1943. Large wartime savings will maintain consumer expenditures somewhat above the level that would otherwise be expected.

- June 18, 1945

RECENT TRENDS IN INDUSTRIAL ACTIVITY

The seasonally adjusted index of industrial production for May was 227 1/; nearly 2 percent under the previous month and 4 percent below May 1944. Production of durable manufactures in May 1945 was the smallest since November 1942, and was 8 percent under May 1944. In contrast, production of nondurable manufactures, although slightly smaller in May than in the first quarter of 1945, was slightly larger than in May 1944. The output of minerals has remained relatively stable since January 1944, although there was a slight decline in May.

The number of workers employed in industry in April 1945 was the smallest since June 1942. The index of 151 2/ for April was 7 percent under a year earlier and 12 percent below the peak reached in November 1943. Most of the decrease occurred in factory employment, although the percentage decline in mining was somewhat larger than in manufacturing. The number of railroad workers in April 1945 was nearly 2 percent greater than a year earlier. Declines in industrial employment during the next few months are likely to be concentrated in a few industries manufacturing war goods.

The seasonally adjusted index of the wage income of industrial workers for April 1945 was 310 3/. This is nearly 3 percent below the previous month and 8 percent under the wartime peak of 335 reached in Feburary 1944. Wage income per employed industrial worker reached a peak in January 1945 when the index was 207. The index for April was slightly lower but 2 percent above a year earlier. The index of the cost of living in large cities rose about 2 percent from April 1944 to April 1945. Income per employed worker is

1/ Federal Reserve Board, 1935-39 = 100.
2/ 1935-39 = 100.
3/ 1935-39 = 100.

likely to decline during the last half of this year, as overtime is reduced following cutbacks in contracts for war goods.

Consumer expenditures for goods and services reached a new high during the first quarter of 1945. The seasonally adjusted index of 176 for the quarter was 8.5 percent above a year earlier and 3.5 percent above the last quarter of 1944. Expenditures for goods have increased more rapidly than those for services. About 10 percent more was spent for goods in the first quarter of 1945 than in the corresponding period of 1944, compared with an increase of 5 percent for services.

The seasonally adjusted index of sales of retail stores for March 1945 was 196 1/, the highest of record and 10 percent above March 1944. After adjusting for the effect of price changes, the index was 142, likewise the highest of record, but only about 7 percent above a year earlier. Approximately two-thirds of the increase in sales over the past year has resulted from increases in the physical quantity of goods sold and changes in the quality and kinds of merchandise handled.

AGRICULTURAL PRICES

The general level of prices received by farmers in June was not much different from that of May, and the index is likely to remain comparatively stable for the rest of 1945. However, later in the year, prices of certain products may decline somewhat. Truck crop prices probably will decline seasonally, and prices of hard wheat of low protein content are likely to be somewhat lower because of the large supply. Prices of nearly all livestock and livestock products will remain at ceiling levels.

The index of prices received by farmers for May was 200 2/, 3 points below the previous month but 6 points above May 1944. The decline from April to May was largely the result of a 66 point decline in the index of truck crop prices, following a sharp increase in April.

Prices paid by farmers have been largely stabilized for more than a year, and this stability seems likely to continue for the remainder of 1945.

FARM INCOME

Total cash receipts from farm marketings in July may be from 5 to 10 percent higher than in June. Hog slaughter will probably be down less than seasonally, because a large proportion of the fall pigs have been held for heavier weights. It is expected that income from wheat, vegetables, and fruit will show about the usual gains. Cash receipts from crops may rise about 40 percent over June, but income from livestock and livestock products probably will drop slightly.

Income in August may increase over July by 10 or 15 percent. If the weather continues favorable, cash receipts from cotton and tobacco will make large seasonal gains. The increase in slaughter of cattle and calves will start in July and will continue in August.

1/ Department of Commerce, 1935-39 = 100.
2/ August 1909 to July 1914 = 100.

Cash receipts from farm marketings in June may add up to about 1,530 million dollars, 5 percent above May, and slightly above June 1944. Income from livestock and livestock products is up slightly above May instead of making the usual decline. Slaughter of meat animals is making moderate gains, and dairy production, which reached a record peak for the month in May, is increasing seasonally.

Cash receipts from crops in June may be about 10 percent over May. There is a substantial increase in income from fruits, as peaches are moving onto markets at about twice the volume of last year and large quantities of cherries, apricots, plums, and prunes are being sold at ceiling prices, while income from citrus fruit is being maintained at about the May level. In spite of backward weather in most vegetable-growing sections, volume of principal truck crop varieties as well as prices are on the whole as high as in May or higher, and cash receipts from vegetables are showing no significant change. Income from food grains is increasing sharply in June as harvesting of the record winter wheat crop advances, although wheat marketing is still being seriously curtailed because of the severe car shortage.

Total cash receipts from farm marketings during the first half year amounted to about 8,710 million dollars, slightly above the income of 8,669 million dollars in 1944. Monthly cash receipts in 1945 have been running very close to the levels for comparable months last year. Increased income from nearly all principal crops largely because of greater quantities carried over from the previous year resulted in a gain of 16 percent in receipts from crops in the first 6 months compared with 1944. Sales of most varieties of meat animals and other livestock products were as great as last year, but marketings of hogs dropped sharply and cash receipts from all livestock and livestock products fell about 7 percent.

LIVESTOCK AND MEATS

Prices of meat animals probably will be maintained at or near present high levels through the remainder of 1945 and in early 1946. Demand for meat is expected to continue strong, and the supply will continue to be less than the record supply in late 1943 and early 1944.

The index of prices received by farmers for meat animals in mid-May was 217 (August 1909-July 1914 = 100), compared with 215 a month earlier and 201 a year earlier. The index of meat animal prices was 1 point higher than in May 1943 and was the highest for the month since 1919. The average price received by farmers for hogs in mid-May was $14.10 per 100 pounds, unchanged from a month earlier, but $1.40 higher than a year earlier. The average price received for beef cattle was $12.90, which was 20 cents higher than a month earlier and 90 cents higher than a year earlier. The average price received by farmers for lambs was $13.50 in mid-May, 40 cents lower than a month earlier, but 10 cents higher than a year earlier.

During early June the beef, pork, and lamb set-asides for Government purchase were slightly reduced, but the armed forces continued to buy heavily. Civilian meat supplies continued very short in many areas, with poor distribution. Cold-storage holdings of meat continued at record low levels.

Meat production in the latter half of 1945 probably will be 5 to 7 percent below the same period a year earlier. Production in the last quarter of the year may be only slightly lower than in the same quarter of 1944. Apparantly, production of all meats during the first half of this year was about 12 percent below a year earlier. All of the reduction in meat output during the first half of this year was in pork. Cattle and calf slaughter was higher than the record slaughter for the period a year earlier. Sheep and lamb slaughter was a record for the season, with ewe slaughter accounting for most of the increase over 1944.

During the last half of 1945 cattle slaughter probably will be larger than a year earlier. Grass cattle marketings through the rest of the year are expected to be relatively large, as farmers and ranchmen are tending to reduce numbers of breeding stock. Slaughter of cows and heifers represented 48 percent of the total cattle slaughtered under Federal inspection during the first 4 months of 1945, compared with 43 percent for the corresponding period of both 1943 and 1944. The early spring movement of cattle to feed lots was relatively large. Shipments of stocker and feeder cattle and calves to 8 Corn Belt States in April and May totaled 232,069 head, 46 percent greater than a year earlier. Shipments of cattle to feed in these States during the first 5 months of the year totaled 531,357 head, 35 percent more than in the corresponding period of 1944, but 6 percent less than the large shipments during the first 5 months of 1943. Most of the cattle going to feed are being fed for a comparatively short period. A direct subsidy of 50 cents per 100 pounds to sellers of good to prime slaughter cattle, beginning May 19, will offer some inducement for increased grain feeding of cattle and increased sales of high-grade grass cattle for slaughter.

Hog slaughter throughout the summer will be far below that of a year earlier, reflecting the 34 percent decrease in the 1944 fall pig crop. Slaughter during the fall and winter probably will be moderately smaller than a year ago because of the smaller pig crop this spring than the 55.4 million saved in the spring of 1944. A continued favorable hog-corn price ratio, and a prospective above-average carryover of feed grains at the end of this feeding year is likely to result in a larger pig crop next fall than the 31.3 million pigs saved in the fall of 1944, which was the smallest since 1940. The increase will largely depend upon the development of this year's corn crop. With a larger fall pig crop in 1945 than in 1944 and a continued large slaughter of cattle and calves, meat production in the late spring and summer of 1946 is likely to be moderately larger than in the corresponding period of this year.

DAIRY PRODUCTS

A record milk production has resulted in large supplies of fluid milk. WFO 79, which limits the sales of fluid milk and cream by distributors and dealers in 138 metropolitan market areas, has been relaxed for the spring and summer months, so that fluid milk consumption is probably at a record rate. Also, the fluid cream conservation aspects of the order have been liberalized from those in effect during the summer of 1944, and consumption of fluid cream is ahead of last year, although below pre-war levels.

Demand for dairy products will continue strong at least through 1945 and early 1946, reflecting high consumer income and large noncivilian takings. Government procurement of Cheddar cheese and evaporated milk will probably amount to about one-half of the yearly output of those products. Even though production of whole milk manufactured dairy products (cheese, evaporated and condensed milk, and dried whole milk) will be at or near record levels, supplies will not be sufficient to meet the demand. Creamery butter output is running below last year and the set-aside at present is higher than last year. However, there appears to be a better regional distribution of civilian butter supplies than in 1944.

Prices received by farmers for the remainder of 1945 and the first part of 1946 will be nearly the same as in 1944. Since December 1942, prices received by dairy farmers have fluctuated within the range of $3.03 to $3.39 per hundred pounds of whole milk, and 49.2 cents to 51.3 cents per pound of butterfat. Wholesale prices of butter have remained unchanged at ceiling levels for 18 months and wholesale prices of Cheddar cheese have been unchanged for 32 months. However, the dairy products-feed price relationship will continue favorable for the dairy enterprise into the first quarter of 1946, partly because of higher dairy production payments rates than in 1944.

Milk production for the first 5 months in 1945 totaled 50.9 billion pounds, 1.7 billion pounds above 1944, and an all-time high for January-May. Continuation of a high rate of production into the first part of 1946 is in prospect, if weather is average or better.

POULTRY AND EGGS

The unusually tight situation in egg supplies probably will continue at least until the fourth quarter of 1945. Egg supplies available for civilians during the latter half of 1945 will be about 20 percent less than during the first half. Although there are upward seasonal adjustments in ceiling prices of eggs, demand will exceed supply mainly because of the scarcity of meat and high consumer incomes. Prices received by farmers probably will reach the highest level for World War II in the second half of 1945, and will be materially higher than in the second half of 1944, when they averaged 37.7 cents a dozen.

Demand for eggs is expected to continue strong into the first part of 1946. Production during the first half of 1946 probably will be about the same as in 1945. However, prospects are for relatively larger meat supplies during the spring and summer of 1946. If this should materialize, some easing in the demand for eggs may occur and prices, by the summer of 1946, may be lower than in corresponding months of 1945.

Demand for poultry meat will continue to exceed supplies at least into early 1946, reflecting the scarcity of red meats, favorable consumer income and large Army procurement. Prices received by farmers in mid-May were 26.6 cents per pound, the highest in over 2 decades. War Food Administration reported wholesale poultry prices in New York City from 30 to 50 percent above permitted ceiling levels.

Production of eggs on farms during the first 5 months of 1945 totaled 2,372 million dozen, 7 percent below that of last year but otherwise the highest on record for the period. Chicks and young chickens on farms June 1 were 1 percent above that of last year. Based on past relationships, the number of hens and pullets on farms January 1, 1946 probably will be about the same as o[n] January 1, 1945.

FATS, OILS, AND OILSEEDS

No substantial relief of the shortage in fats and oils is in prospect before spring or summer of 1946. By that time supplies of food fats may be increased somewhat by an increase in lard production (from 1945 fall pigs) over the present level; imports of copra may be available from the Philippines and the present tight linseed oil situation may be relieved by imports of flaxseed, if the 1945-46 Argentine crop is of normal size. Also, the period of most acute European need for imports of food probably will be over when the new harvest begins in the summer of 1946.

Military requirements for fats and oils probably will be smaller in 194[6] than in 1945, as a result of reductions in the size of the armed forces and in the number of prisoners. Consumer income is likely to be reduced somewhat in 1946. However, civilian supplies of most fats and oils probably will continue to be smaller than the quantity consumers are able and willing to pay for at the present level of prices.

Stocks of fats and oils are now lowest for the season in many years, an[d] probably will continue to decline until crushing of 1945 crops of oilseeds gets under way in volume this fall. This is a result of reduced production of fats and oils this year and continued large military and export requirement[s]. Factory and warehouse stocks of fats and oils on April 30, the latest reporte[d] date, totaled 1,822 million pounds (crude basis) compared with 1,895 million pounds a month earlier and 2,601 million pounds a year earlier, when lard was piling up in storage. The principal reductions from April 30 last year to the corresponding date this year were in lard, inedible tallow and greases, linseed oil, and soybean oil.

Average prices to farmers for soybeans, flaxseed, and peanuts were 2 to 12 percent higher in mid-May than a year earlier, reflecting higher support and ceiling prices. Cottonseed prices, however, were slightly lower. The mid-May averages this year were as follows: cottonseed, $52.10 per ton; peanuts, $8.30 cents per pound; soybeans, $2.15 per bushel; flaxseed, $2.91 per bushel.

CORN AND OTHER FEED

Price prospects for feed grains for the 1945-46 season depend to a con siderable extent upon outturn of the corn crop. A large production of oats b[ut] a reduced production of barley is indicated for 1945. An high level of demand in prospect for livestock and livestock products, for industrial grain produc[ts] and for feed concentrates for export. This, together with Government loan pr[o] grams on feed grains, will tend to maintain feed grain prices at a relativel[y] high level during most of the 1945-46 season, although large feed crops in 1945 could result in somewhat lower prices than in the present season.

A strong demand for byproduct feeds is holding terminal market prices of those feeds at or near ceilings. Feed mixers and livestock producers continue to take the current production of byproduct feeds as rapidly as it becomes available. Prices of almost all byproduct feeds have been at about ceiling levels for 2 years. Average farm prices of feed grains and hay are below ceilings, but prices of best grades of feed grains at primary markets are at ceilings.

As a result of excessive rainfall and cool weather over large areas during April and May, feed prospects on June 1 were not so favorable as a month or two ago. Acreage planted to corn is expected to be somewhat smaller than last year, But a larger carry-over of corn is in prospect than in 1944, so that the total supply of corn for 1945-46 may compare favorably with the large 1944-45 supply. Barley production for 1945 is indicated to be almost 258 million bushels, 9 percent smaller than in 1944, and the smallest since 1938. The 1945 production of oats is indicated at 1,334 million bushels, 14 percent more than in 1944 and the second largest in 20 years. This year's hay crop (including tame and wild hay) may total about 97 million tons. A crop this size would be smaller than those of the last 3 years, but larger than any other since 1927.

The total number of grain-consuming animal units on farms next January 1 probably will not be greatly different from the number on January 1, 1945. With average growing conditions during the remainder of the season, the 1945-46 supply of feed grains probably would be adequate for the indicated domestic livestock, food, and industrial requirements.

WHEAT

Ceiling prices were revised upward 3-1/8 cents, effective May 30. The price of hard wheat of high protein as well as soft red wheat moved up to the new ceiling levels. There is too little of these types in old crop supplies to satisfy current mill demands. The price of hard wheats of low protein showed no response to the ceiling revision, and in fact, dropped slightly. This was due in considerable measure to the expanding movement of new crop wheat in Texas and Oklahoma.

During the harvest period, wheat prices at terminal markets may be expected to fall only moderately below ceiling levels. Of the hard wheats, those of low protein test will drop relatively more than those of higher test. Prices in terminal markets, however, will continue to be supported by exceptionally large military and War Food Administration purchases as well as substantial pruchase for industrial alchhol production, and by the probability that a shortage of cars will limit the quantity of wheat which can move to market. Price declines at local markets may be larger than at terminals, because of insufficient cars to move the large crop in prospect. The car situation has been improving, but it is not probable that car numbers will be adequate early in the season.

Loan rates on the 1945 crop, announced May 30 and reflecting 90 percent of parity, are based on a national average of approximately $1.38 a bushel on the farm. The rates were predicated on the May 15 wheat parity of $1.53 a bushel. If the parity price of wheat advanced more than 1 cent a bushel before July 1, an adjustment will be made in the rates. With current prices more than 5 cents above the loan basis, and with some apprehension over the car situation, farmers are free sellers of the newly harvested crop.

The 1945 wheat production was indicated at 1,085 million bushels, based on June 1 conditions. If a crop of this size is realized it would top last year's record slightly, and would be the third U. S. crop of over a billion bushels. The movement of grain to ports for export has exceeded earlier expectations, and it now appears that the carry-over on July 1, 1945, may not be greatly different from the 316 million bushels a year earlier. Prospective large exports, continued large takings by the military forces, and utilization for industrial alcohol, in addition to food and feed requirements, may result in the total disappearance being about equal to the large crop in prospect. Accordingly, the carry-over July 1, 1946 may be about the same as on July 1, 1945.

Spring work in Canada was delayed by too much moisture, but seeding was practically completed by June 1. Warm weather has subsequently been needed to promote germination and growth. The drought in Australia has been partially broken. Recent rains have fallen in the main wheat areas in time for seeding, but more moisture will be required for current needs and to build up reserves. Weather conditions in Argentina remain favorable for seeding. Crop prospects are below average in Europe, reflecting reduced acreage and a shortage of fertilizers. News from Russia is generally favorable, with acreage greatly increased compared with 1944.

FRUIT

With total market supplies of fresh fruits at a seasonal low level, prices in late May and early June continued strong at or near ceiling levels for all principal fruits except lemons. This generally strong market position of fresh fruits is expected to continue for at least another month. Although market supplies of citrus fruits were declining seasonally while supplies of new-crop deciduous fruits were increasing, supplies of citrus fruits still comprised about three-fourths of the total in early June, judging by carlot shipments.

Prices for oranges at terminal wholesale markets were at or near ceiling levels in late May and early June. Prices for the remaining supplies of Florida oranges, for which the season is now drawing to a close a full month earlier than usual, are expected to continue at ceilings. In the case of California Valencia oranges, which will provide practically all of the fresh oranges from now until fall, prices for the better grades and preferred sizes probably will continue at ceiling levels. But prices for the smaller sizes, of which there is a larger-than-usual percentage this season, may average somewhat below ceilings. Although the supplies of California Valencia oranges remaining to be marketed after the first of June are substantially larger than a year earlier, the remaining supplies of Florida oranges are much smaller, with the consequence that total supplies are only moderately larger than a year earlier. This places California Valencia oranges in a stronger market position than otherwise would be the case.

Terminal market prices for grapefruit in May and early June averaged near ceiling levels, reflecting a strong consumer demand and seasonally decreasing supplies. This strong market position is expected to continue for the remaining supplies, which consist mostly of California-Arizona grapefruit. The season in Texas and Florida is practically over, closing in the latter State more than a month earlier than usual.

Prices for lemons, which were at ceiling levels at terminal markets in April and early May, declined sharply by mid-May, under the impact of large market supplies and weak demand arising no doubt mainly from the generally cool weather. Prices should improve with warmer weather, even though supplies remaining to be marketed after the first of June are substantially larger than a year earlier.

Prices for 1944-crop eastern apples rose slightly during late May and early June in the New York City and Chicago wholesale markets, while Western apples continued to sell at or near ceiling levels. Early apples of the 1945 crop, the market movement of which is just getting under way and will continue through August, are expected to sell at or near ceilings, in view of the very short crops of early varieties in all States except California. Ceiling prices for 1945-crop early apples have been raised by 68 cents a bushel (from $2.85 to $3.53), effective for the period May 29 through June 20, 1945, because of decreased yields (MPR 426, Amdt. 108). Although a very short crop of all commercial apples is in prospect in the eastern two-thirds of the United States conditions point to a crop that is average or slightly larger in the Western States.

Terminal market prices for new-crop cherries and peaches were at ceiling levels in late May and early June. They are expected to decline the second half of June, in accordance with scheduled decreases in ceiling prices (MPR 426, Amdts. 101 and 102). The recently announced ceiling prices for the 1945 crops of these two fruits are intended to permit the same national average returns to growers as was intended through the maximum prices in force for the 1944 crops. Based on June 1 conditions, the indicated production this year compared with last is substantially larger for California prunes, slightly larger for sweet cherries and peaches, about the same for pears, and substantially smaller for sour cherries and apricots.

TRUCK CROPS

Commercial Truck Crops For Fresh Market

The generally downward movement of prices paid to farmers for truck crops for fresh market experienced during May has extended into June, and prices for practically all fresh market truck crops are expected to continue to decline seasonally well into the summer. The weighted average wholesale price of 14 important vegetables on the New York market for the week ended June 2, 1945 was about 8 percent lower than for the week ended May 5, 1945, although about 2 percent higher than for the week ended June 3, 1944.

Unseasonably cold, wet weather in May and early June retarded development of crops in most areas, and persistent dry weather has reduced crop prospects in the extreme southeastern United States, particularly in Florida. Nevertheless, the aggregate tonnage of commercial truck crops for harvest this spring is still indicated to be slightly above a year ago and about one-fifth above the 10-year 1934-43 average spring tonnage. Early estimates covering approximately one-half of the total summer production point to a possible tonnage of these crops 5 percent greater than comparable 1944 production and about one-sixth larger than the 10-year (1934-43) average. Compared with last year, heavier supplies in the early summer period of this year are expected for beets, cabbage, cantaloups, grean peppers and watermelon lighter supplies are expected for snap beans, celery, cucumbers, lettuce, onion and tomatoes.

Commercial Truck Crops
For Processing

The aggregate acreage planted to 11 important truck crops for commercial processing in 1945 is expected to be about 5 percent larger than the aggregate 1944 planting. If intentions are carried out, processors will have the production from a record-high acreage to can, freeze, pickle or otherwise process in 1945.

Total needs for canned vegetables continue at a high level. Because of high military requirements, the per capita supply of canned vegetables for civilians in the pack year 1945-46 may be lower than at any other time in the past 10 years, and about one-eighth smaller than in the current 1944-45 pack year. Military requirements are being assured through the operations of WFO 22.9, which requires processors to set aside and reserve varying proportions of their pack to meet Government requirements. Set-aside percentages for canned asparagus and canned spinach were increased effective May 20, 1945 (WFO 22.9, Amdt. 1), and further amendments affecting other canned vegetables, tomato juice and tomato products are expected.

Support prices and designated prices already announded for 1945 crop vegetables for processing give growers reasonable assurance that the prices they receive for processing crops grown this year will be at about the same levels as last year.

POTATOES AND SWEETPOTATOES

Shipping point f.o.b. prices for new-crop potatoes have remained generally at ceilings so far this season, but declined about 20 cents per 100 pounds in recent weeks, reflecting the scheduled June 1 decline in ceiling prices. Prices may redede somewhat from ceiling levels in July, particularly if shipments from late spring commercial areas--where development of the crop has been delayed by cold weather in May and early June--should come to market at the same time that summer-crop areas are shipping in considerable volume. Carlot shipments of new potatoes by rail and boat averaged close to 5,400 cars per week during the 3 weeks ended June 9 and are expected to continue at a fairly high level through June.

Although unseasonably cold, wet weather delayed maturity and reduced prospective yields in several States, the total commercial early potato crop is indicated to be of record large size. Judging from the active demand for all available surplus seed stocks in some of the northern States, it is possible that total acreages of all potatoes planted in 1945 may exceed the acreage indicated by farmers' intentions in March.

Government pruchases for military requirements continue to be a large factor in the total demand for potatoes. The restrictions of WFO 120 (which requires shippers to offer loadings to Government procurement agencies before they may obtain a permit to ship into civilian markets) were withdrawn May 22 from Maine, the last of the 1944 late-crop potato areas to be freed from its provisions. On the other hand, the WFO 120 restrictions still apply to the new-crop pototoes from Kern County, California, and were extended June 4 to include important early-crop counties of North Carolina and Virginia.

The price-support schedule for 1945 crop early and intermediate potatoes has been revised to include also U. S. No. 1 grade B size and U. S. No. 2 grade. The support price for such grades will be 50 percent of the applicable basis price announced for U. S. No. 1 grade for the area concerned (USDA 914-45).

The price support and loan program for the 1945 late crop, announced May 18, 1945, largelyl follows the schedule for the 1944 crop, and provides support for all potatoes U. S. No. 2 grade, 1-7/8 inch minimum, or better. Principal reliance is placed on the loan program, though purchase and diversion programs will be used when necessary where loans are not feasible (USDA 913-45). To fill a gap in the schedule as announced May 18, a June 6 announcement dded a support price for July 1945 for the State of Washington.

A few cars of 1944 crop sweetpotatoes were still being shipped in early June, as the new 1945 crop began moving. Prices continue at ceilings, reflecting an active demand and the seasonal low point in market supplies. The 1945 crop ceiling prices will be 17 cents per bushel above the previous year and are designed to reflect a season average return of $2.75 per bushel, f.o.b. the basing point, Sunset, Louisiana. The ceiling prices in effect on the 1944 crop of sweetpotatoes ranged from $1.90 per bushel during the main harvesting season to a high of $3.15 late in the storage season, and averaged $2.58 per bushel at the same basing point. This year's price action has been taken to stimulate increased production to meet greater needs.

COTTON

During the month ended June 15, the 10-market price of Middling 15/16-inch cotton averaged 22.71 cents per pound. This was 32 points higher than a month earlier when it averaged 22.39 cents per pound, and 147 points higher than during the comparable period last season. The actual daily prices fluctuated between 22.53 and 22.82 and compare with an average parity equivalent for the 10 markets as of May 15 of 22.61 cents per pound, an average Government purchase price of 22.36, and a Government domestic sales price of 22.76 cents per pound.

In May domestic mills consumed nearly 831,000 bales of cotton. This is equivalent to an annual rate of almost 9.5 million bales. This is slightly lower than in April or the average for the season to date and the lowest since last October. For the season to date (10 months), consumption has totaled 8.1 million bales, 300,000 bales or 3.5 percent less than during the comparable period last season. The continuation of consumption in June and July at the same level as in May, would result in a total consumption this season of about 9.7 million bales.

The cotton textile situation for a number of months has been such that the armed forces have had to make certain substitutions, such as accepting tent twill where they were unable to obtain as much duck as they desired. Neither the civilians in this country nor the exporters have been able to obtain anything like all of the cotton textiles they desired. This occurs despite the abundant total supply of raw cotton, mainly because of the unfavorable labor situation with which cotton mills are confronted. The scarcity of textiles for civilians and for export is expected to continue at least until after VJ-Day. Should there be any increase in total cotton textile production before the end of 1945, as is at least a possibility, the supply of textiles available for civilians and for export would probably increase, inasmuch as no net increase in military takings is in prospect. Just how long it will be before the demand for textiles drops sufficiently to bring about a reduction in cotton textile production remains to be seen. However, demand will be maintained at least until sometine after VJ-Day.

The new crop appears to have improved materially in early June, after having been delayed by excessive moisture and subnormal temperatures. Reports from most areas of the Belt indicate boll weevil numbers sufficient to cause heavy damage unless control measures (poisoning) and hot and dry weather hold them in check.

WOOL

The average price received by farmers for wool in May was 41.0 cents a pound. This compares with 40.4 cents in April, and a revised average of 42.8 cents in May 1944. The average price to growers this year now seems likely to be lower than the 1944 weighted average of 42.4 cents a pound (grease basis). As the CCC is supporting the 1945 clip at clean prices which are substantially the same as in 1944, the lower prices to growers this year probably are due largely to differences in the quality and shrinkage of the wools.

Mill demand for domestic wool has increased, compared with last year, owing to larger production of military fabrics. CCC sales of domestic wool during the first 4 months of 1945 totaled approximately 100 million pounds, grease basis, about twice as much as in the correspondin period last year. Total United States mill use of apparel wool in 1945 probably will not differ much from the 1944 consumption of 1 billion pounds grease basis. Production of military fabrics in 1945, however, will be considerably larger than the 1944 production, and this should provide an outlet for a much larger quantity of domestic wool this year than last. CCC sales of domestic wool in 1944 totaled approximately 235 million pounds, grease basis, compared with the 1944 domestic production of 418 million pounds.

The 1945 clip is now moving rapidly to appraisal centers. Through June 16 about 74 million pounds of shorn wool had been appraised for CCC purchase under the 1945 purchase program. This was somewhat less than the quantity of 1944 shorn wool appraised to the corresponding date last year.

Stocks of apparel wool held by mills and dealers and by the United States Government on April 1, 1945 were about 70 million pounds smaller than a year earlier, when reported stocks totaled 745 million pounds. April 1 stocks of domestic wool--largely owned by the CCC--were about 100 million pounds larger this year than a year earlier. But the increase in stocks of domestic wool was more than offset by a decline of approximately 210 million pounds in stocks of foreign wool owned by the DSC. Mills and dealers held larger stocks of foreign wool on April 1 this year than last. The reported stocks of domestic wool do not include any appreciable quantity of the new clip, since little new clip wool had moved from farms and ranches by April 1.

TOBACCO

Demand for Maryland tobacco, the only type now being marketed by farmers, continues strong, with prices of most grades except nondescript at the 57-cent ceiling established for the 1944 crop. So far this season, the poorest grade of Maryland sold on the auction markets has averaged 18 cents per pound. Through June 22, net sales for the season on auction markets totaled approximately 19 million pounds at an average of almost 55 cents per pound, as compared with 46 cents for the corresponding period last year, and the record high of 56 cents for the 1942 crop.

Practically all of the 1944 crop of cigar tobacco has been sold by growers at or near the established ceilings. It appears that the season average price for the 1944 crop of cigar tobacco will be about the same as for the 1943 crop, inasmuch as the ceilings for the various individual types are approximately the same.

Despite the all-time high level of disappearance, stocks of flue-cured and burley are expected to be somewhat larger on July 1, 1945 than a year earlier, because of the exceptionally large 1944 crop. Cigarette manufacturers purchased more tobacco in the 1944-45 marketing season than they withdrew from stored stocks. In view of the favorable prospects for another large crop this year, supplies of cigarette tobacco, particularly burley, may be considerably larger in 1945-46 than in 1944-45. Flue-cured and burley acreage allotments for each year since 1940 have been larger than the preceding year, and the allotments for 1945 are more than 50 percent greater than the 1940 allotments. Flue-cured markets are scheduled to open July 24 in the Georgia-Florida area for sale of this 1945 crop.

Production of cigarettes is continuing at or near record levels. Domestic consumption during the 1944-45 fiscal year was about 9 percent below 1943-44, but shipments abroad were considerably larger. Consumption of snuff, chewing tobacco and smoking tobacco is continuing at peak levels for the war period. Domestic cigar consumption is above a year ago, but it is still at an exceptionally low level.

ECONOMIC TRENDS AFFECTING AGRICULTURE

Item	Unit of base period	1944 Year	1944 May.	1945 Feb.	1945 Mar.	1945 Apr.	1945 May.
Industrial Production 1/	1935-39						
Total	=100	235	236	236	235	231	227
All manufactures	"	252	253	253	252	247	242
Durable goods	"	353	357	347	345	336	327
Nondurable goods	"	171	169	176	176	174	174
Minerals	"	140	143	141	142	140	138
Construction activity 1/	1935-39						
Contracts, total	=100	73	58	103	125	122	105
Contracts, residential	"	39	39	32	37	44	51
Wholesale prices 2/	1935-39						
All commodities 1	= 100	129	129	131	131	131	132
All commodities except farm and food	"	121	121	122	122	122	122
Farm products	"	162	162	167	167	170	171
Food	"	133	133	132	132	134	135
Prices received and paid by farmers 3/	1910-14 =100						
Prices received, all prod.	"	195	194	199	198	203	200
Prices paid, int. and taxes	"	170	169	172	173	173	173
Parity ratio	"	115	115	116	114	117	116
Cost of living 5/	1935-39						
Total	=100	126	125	127	127	127	128
Food	"	136	136	136	136	137	139
Non food	"	120	120	122	122	122	122
Income	1935-39						
Nonagricultural payments 4/	=100	231	229	240	240	238	---
Cash farm 3/	"	265	276	312	294	296	293
Income of Industrial Workers 3/	"	325	327	320	318	310	---
Factory payrolls 5/	"	356	356	350	346	338	---
Weekly earnings of factory workers 5/	Dollars						
All manufacturing	"	46.08	46.02	47.43	47.43	47.16	---
Durable goods	"	52.07	51.89	53.39	53.25	52.99	---
Nondurable goods	"	37.12	37.03	38.73	38.95	38.81	---
Employment							
Total civilian 6/	Millions	51.8	52.0	50.6	50.8	51.2	51.3
Employees in nonagri. est. 5/	Thous.	36,682	38,672	37,957	38,062	37,804	37,654
Farm 3/	"	10037	10068	8051	8,414	8982	10017
Government finance (Federal) 7/	Mil. dol						
Receipts, net	"	3,702	2,950	3,767	6,892	2,929	3,085
Expenditures	"	8,097	8,292	7,460	9,433	7,968	9,275

Sources: 1/ Federal Reserve Board; converted to a 1935-39 base. 2/ U. S. Dept. Labor, B. L. S, 3/ U. S. Dept. of Agriculture, B. A. E. To convert prices recei and prices paid, interest and taxes to the 1935-39 base, multiply by .93110 and .78125 reppectively. 4/ U. S. Dept. of Commerce. 5/ U. S. Dept. of Labor, B. I 6/ U. S. Dept. of Commerce, Bureau of the Census. 7/ U. S. Dept. of Treasury. Data for 1944 are on average monthly basis.

Lightning Source UK Ltd.
Milton Keynes UK
UKHW010656211218
334353UK00007B/99/P